# Fort Necessity

PHOENIX POETS

DAVID GEWANTER

# *Fort Necessity*

THE UNIVERSITY OF CHICAGO PRESS
Chicago & London

The University of Chicago Press, Chicago 60637
The University of Chicago Press, Ltd., London
© 2018 by The University of Chicago
Published 2018

27  26  25  24  23  22  21  20  19  18      1  2  3  4  5

ISBN-13: 978-0-226-53376-6 (paper)
ISBN-13: 978-0-226-53393-3 (e-book)
DOI: https://doi.org/10.7208/chicago/9780226533933.001.0001

Library of Congress Cataloging-in-Publication Data

Names: Gewanter, David, author.
Title: Fort Necessity / David Gewanter.
Other titles: Phoenix poets.
Description: Chicago ; London : The University of Chicago Press,
    2018. | Series: Phoenix poets
Identifiers: LCCN 2017056779 | ISBN 9780226533766 (pbk. : alk.
    paper) | ISBN 9780226533933 (e-book)
Subjects: LCSH: Working class—Poetry.
Classification: LCC PS3557.E897 F678 2018 | DDC 811/.54—dc23
LC record available at https://lccn.loc.gov/2017056779

*~ for James ~*


*"you and me was ever friends"*

*—Dickens*

```
            WORK
           /      \
    MAKES        BREAKS
           \      /
        VESSEL-BODY
```

THE SPEEDUP
"reach under, adjust washer, screw down bolt . . .
Reachunderadjustscrewdownreachunderadjust"

—John Dos Passos, *The Big Money*

# CONTENTS

# ACKNOWLEDGMENTS

Thanks to the editors of magazines who published these poems:

*Agni Online*: "The Coin Purse"
*Poetry International*: "'Second Eden'" and "Fort Necessity" (first section)
*Ploughshares*: "Wellfleet: Off-Season"
*Smartish Pace*: "Old Egg"
*Tikkun*: "The Lords of Labor"
*Western Humanities Review*: "Day, Week, Month, Year" (part of "Fort Necessity")

Thanks to these generous friends, in whose summer homes I read and wrote: Phyllis Lee Levin; Connie Casey and Harold Varmus; Susan Dacey and Bruce Daniel; and Sarah Blake and Josh Weiner. Many friends read and helped the poems: Barbara F. T., Bob H., Dennis T., Duncan W., Jane B., Jennifer F., John S., Jon R., Kerry W., Mary-Sherman W., Maureen C., Michael C., Nathan H., Pam R., Tom S., and especially Josh and Joy and Randy. Georgetown University kindly supported a semester's leave and trip to Fort Necessity, PA, and to the Homestead factory site.

# THE COIN PURSE

She said: I always talk against my chances,
paint a picture of what I want
   and show the ways I won't get it—

I fill up a room of desires,
tally all the pieces there,
   and then, like the moving man

carry out the cargo. Such *freedom*.
When it's empty—that is,
   when I see my listener's

eyes drop, finding the room
cleaned out, the dusty air
   and echoing voice, then I click

the conversation off,
snap it like a little coin purse.
   I hoard my luck.

I

"Go, get you home, you fragments"

—*Coriolanus*

# OLD EGG

"To peel away at people, to leave them raw, exposed—
that's what movies do: like King Lear's servant
dragged from the banquet, and thrown in the stocks;
    winking, the hostess tells

her husband, *Nay, my Lord, leave him all night too*
and pulls off the man's boots . . . . Well, in my movie,
there's a neglected wife who envies her friend
    dating online—

So her friend signs her up for a date. Her husband?
His pal cheats on his wife, internet hook-ups: and so
he signs up the husband too. The wife agrees to one date;
    so does her husband,

and that's the first two acts of the script.
In the third act, of course, there's a mistake:
they're set up with each other and, surprise,
    they meet at the bar:

what happens next: a slap, a break-up, or fresh sex?
Push at the calcified shell of marriage: pressure,
a crack; more pressure, then it breaks open.
    —But no magic ending,

not like the poet watching the film of his parents
courting—He wept for them to stop, but the audience
hushed him: *the future's already happened,*
*and you're inside it.*"

# HOUSE AND FORTUNE

His childhood home was angry,
screams and curses bounced off
windows and walls, and soaked
into wood and lath plaster.

The house flexed after his father left,
after the snarling divorce;
the walls repainted, mother remarried—
But it had suckled too long,

and still breathed back their rage.
He escaped at last, then carried
a memory-room forty years.
    Now, inside his own house,

he ducks trouble with his wife
(house made quiet in fear of echoes)—
Then his folks come to his daughter's party:
still feuding, they can't share a room.

He parks his father on the patio,
tows his mother to the kitchen;
the two old jalopies, who fueled
each other in love and hate,

stay in their ruts. The party buzzes on,
the house pulse steady . . . till he sees them
shuffle to the bathroom door
and wait there: chatting and listening.

*After all this grief,* he hisses,
*they're using my house to fix things?*
He feels, somehow, betrayed—
an upside-down feeling, but true:

his little room tips, and all
the treasures of bitterness spill out.
Wooden timbers bend;
his house drinks at the source.

## WELLFLEET, OFF-SEASON

The doctors do not read the sea, or the grindstone beach; swaddled in holiday hats and sunglasses, they doze like ancient directors on the set, while salt-air and neeptide winds gently abrade the flesh, until their ash of illness crumbles and

drifts away, miseries given back to nature each August—motes for the crab to pick, mulch for the beach-flower—until, scrubbed clean, the aged ozone-babies return to their cities, ready for another year.

Now, in November, the beach performs for no one, a soup of rock and water waiting for August, washing itself absently—

Exhalations rise through cold air; clouds twist like rags, like lancets or gauze. No heroic gestures. Just headless statues of mist, darkening as their bellies grow.

*"A late evening in the future"*
—Beckett


He hauled a hundred voices home,
spun the little dramas of the day
into gnarled and freakish arias
    to lift her at dinner

or, sleepy in bed, he'd turn and whisper
like Pepé Le Pew: *En garde,*
*leetle cupcahke! My lips,*
    *zey approach you . . . .*

But later, once the hectic jokes had leapt
upon the last ones, strangling them
in the quiet comfort of the house,
    then her face

relaxed into a smooth deadness,
became a Buddha of calm suffering—
now, even his practiced pranks
    left her silent,

his finger puppet show of Dick
Cheney in Hell, or the fast gag,
"A dyslexic walks into a bra" . . .
    his stories thinned down,

the stage-furniture fading away
until every speaker sounded the one
flat tone of smirking mockery,
    removed from

the world, voice of superb disdain
jabbing at the teller, rattling
the grate; the ghost voice of
    actors like

George Raft or George Sanders,
failed romantics who grew to hate
their own weaknesses—so that Sanders's
    suicide note

read like the end of a jaunty marriage:
*Dear World: I am leaving*
*because I am bored.*
    *Good luck.*

# RUTH, THE ROCKET

(RG, 1916–2013)

Like a brown brioche crumbling at the rim,
the dying motherlode of plutonium-238
fuels the Cassini spacecraft through
the solar hinterlands. After blastoff, it would
    slingshot round Venus,

fly close by Earth again, then race
the Jovian magnet. Destination Saturn.
At 46,000 mph, it was a killer-boomerang,
"A nuke aimed at Earth" the protesters
    cry, marching behind

bagpipers to Cape Canaveral.
Police in riot gear open razor gates,
escorting an 87-year-old lady
into custody. *You go Granny!*
    They clamber up fences

and drop into the arms
of deputies. Watching this on TV
and spoiling for a fight, is Grandma Ruth:
she flips through her protest signs,
    IMPEACH JOHNSON!

IMPEACH NIXON! & FORD! IMPEACH REAGAN!
BEAT BACK BUSH! (But not Bill Clinton:
"husbands who fool around don't start wars.")
Her new placard, HELL NO, WE WON'T GLOW!,
    ready to wave

at the White House. But how sleepless
are the engineers of space, the unlaid and
unblinking clockwatchers—they snatch up
the DC parade permit for that day,
      and march in

      figure-eights, showing support for Cassini
and infinity, leaving the Death Ship legions
to bicker from the sidewalks. Blocked from
assaulting the White House, Ruth takes
      a tour of it instead

("very interesting"), then two days touring
the Holocaust Museum ("very interesting")
as Cassini, the menacing skull of wonders,
abstract of the bodiless brain, rockets through
      the sky palace . . . .

      Nuclear brioche 238,
baked in iridium and ceramic casings,
would only "break like cups and plates,"
not sprinkle mortal dust on Disney World.
      Further NASA protection:

"Our safety report is two feet thick."
Years later, Cassini approaches Earth:
its dreaded fly-by. Protests surge again; but now
age has come to Ruth in a thousand rivulets:
      her ankles collapse,

stove left burning, the stairs a Matterhorn.
Alzheimer's is feared, Alzheimer's is tested,
the great No-Face _____.
Sometimes she loses its name too, buoyed
   and floating

   on the still lake of antipsychotics
(tiny dose) to keep her even-tempered
(tiny drift to the waterfall). Ruth,
who once protested power steering,
   now sits through

   doomsday while Cassini, distracted angel,
misses Earth, carrying its cargo deaths
to Saturn, which swims through a seven-year
winter . . . so dark, a banker could not count
   its silver moons.

   As Cassini touches Saturn's storms
and braids, Ruth's ganglia have burnt out:
the roadways through her skull's sockets now
loop inward, a carousel of old furniture
   and phrases.

   She forgets her enemies—an inverted grace—;
moves to the Home of motherloads, reliving
the same day; then the locked ward, Salon of
*Tilted and Recumbent Ladies*, where parents
   become children again,

all saved, and lost.  Saturn also moves
to springtime, its vast, hexagonal
hurricane of ammonia whirling round
the north pole, deep enough to swallow
     four Earths—

How far will Creation retreat?
Grainy images flood back. The bright
curtains of electrical fire crash down
continually at the edges, geysers
     of war-music

     spewing toward Cassini as she loops
the icy loops, dutifully tracing the maze
of her own decay; blackness incurable
as she weakens, salves of Jerusalem
     for her temples

     and wrists, childhood songs flicker her eyelids;
a kiss, and then the oxygen mask
is lifted from the face, hissing and released
from the body in revolt . . . .
     One day

the Sun will swell, and grow through us,
arranging the stars into families of light.

# "SECOND EDEN"

—Thomas Hardy


The blood their parents gave them
    seems like original sin—
hugs and kisses, saliva or cuts
    might pull another child in.

They're careful at the park, for
    carefulness will save them
from spending their inheritance,
    the blood their parents gave them;

but when they come to AIDS camp
    they play and wrestle and run;
no fear of giving infections
    until visitors come.

## STICK THE LANDING

*gymnast Kerri Strug, Olympics 1996*

Because they are tiny and gaunt and strong,
willow spine and sturdy cabled legs,

because they are willful, and drive themselves
like sled dogs, the girls grow in the gym,

on spongy mats and liniment air, stalking
the bars and beams and horses. High above,

a boy hangs from the rings: a pocket-Hercules,
arms rigidly out, face of stone, a kind

of machine-still crucifix . . . yet the muscles
tremble slightly, human and imperfect,

the judges note. His body on trial.
The girls are pixies (though their hands blister)

and live inside a peter pan curse;
our never-grow-up darlings, waving brightly

in track suits, fresh, unstained: no blood on the leg
to announce the woman in the body:

they clutch the last month of girlhood for years.
In the stands loom their sisters, a haunt-eyed

race of elves waiting their turn, picking at
callouses. Little Sandi, Chantelle, Becca,

eager snapping birds. And the massive,
soft-bellied parents, who slosh and jig

at their bony, capering daughters below—
their rocket jumps, arched back and peekaboo,

now puppet, now python; now scissors, or
yoyo—yet all the while, the minute

failings of a hand or knee drop the score from
the crevice of 10. The judges tap, tap:

because they once had leapt, because they coach,
because girlhoods linger in their eyes,

they sit there, girdled, the weird sisters.
Yet their masks did crackle once, and betray

a feeling—just once: in Atlanta,
when Kerri, the littlest of Americans

hurtled toward the horse, ricocheted upward,
twisting and falling . . . yet her body botched

the landing, tore the ankle ligaments,
toppling her back. Mark and stain were tallied.

—hopping to the arms of her bearlike coach,
who whispered in foreign accent: *one more vault,*

*one high score, and we win.* So she ran and jumped,
desperate soldier, arching and spinning . . .

and the feet stuck. But once she turned to
face the judges, she lifted the torn leg

like a faun. Then it was that the judges gaped,
and jerked their hands to their open mouths,

and saw the ruin and the triumph of it all.
After the numbers, after the ribbons

and medals, it was their hands that said:
Judge this child. Judge this childhood,

that broke before you.

THE *EGO* ANTHOLOGY

I. jumble *Ego,*

like a sagging barn, let's say, a barn sagging
with old toys gathered from city streets—
like a hidden doorhandle, a handlebar
mustache, your stash of love letters, the love bite
you gave to your arm; like an armoire
bursting with party clothes, a clothes-horse
you ride naked, ride until you come,
a come-as-you-are party of one,
a party of one hundred cloudy mirrors
that city folk find in the sagging barn,
all the trinkets looking vaguely familiar
like that special poem tucked in the drawer,
the one sent by your old love, remember?
you had said, *this one speaks to me.*

II. service *Ego*:

She sees him shuffle crabwise down the meat aisle—
*Is he that old? Am I?*—years after the years
of analysis. He grips a paper bag
of papers, confused, slowly collapsing
inside the black office suit he wore when
torrents of intimacies had poured down
his gullet, the years of *When he hurts me,*
*I apologize . . .* Load on him the causes,
O Muse. The sausages dangle above him.
She takes his arm: *Doctor, remember me?*
*are you all right?*—Once he had told her,
*You're no fireman. And he's no burning house.*
Now he looks up, the lockbox, the old child
playing doctor: *Oh hello. You can't help me.*


III. last stop *Ego*,

". . . the Berlin Wall came down, the markets opened—
all this killed off downtown Lodz; now our clothes
come from China. Yet after the mills closed,
look! the snow turned white. We never knew.
Old Poles stand in the doorways, staring past you,
selling flowers or forks. Everyone you meet
is drunk: some guy throws a cat, or a baby,
out the window—should we be shocked? Lodz
has two plans to save itself: build an airport
near the highway, or get tourists to visit
the old train station: we were the last stop
before the camps. Everyone goes to Auschwitz,
their hotels are full—not ours. We're building
a memorial, and we've got the cattle cars."

IV. *Ego* rampant,

all grown, toothed and whiskered, a sweaty walrus
of appetites, a towering Samuel Johnson: mutton
and mince at his waistcoats, bird bones snap and fly back
to the plate. Queen Anne had touched his mottled face
but could not cure it of *King's Evil*. His clucks
and whale-breath, his hands jerking like Dr. Strangelove—
How to restore the body? He wrote "Happy Valley"
tales to pay his mother's funeral, found the bookstall
where he had snubbed his father, stood in rain for penance.
Gravities pull at the joints, till the tendons stretch
and sag. Our animal pains distract us from acting
human, as books and company kept Johnson from
staring at Hell, and feeding his old friend, depression:
*My breakfast is solitary, the black dog waits to share it.*


V. *Ego* dust,

as if a tidy Manx housewife would cut
her tattered curtains into tablecloths—
then, years later, sew them up as aprons,
then napkins, then purses, doilies, spice bags,
pincushion. It is not Zen, this slow vanishing,
not *the Will, pouring itself out*—Watch it
shrink inward: the holding cell where drunks dry out;
the orange, wincing on the windowsill,
the dry testicle in its gloom: your heavy
bag of habits, the frozen clothes swinging on
the laundry line, as if to sail somewhere—
pray for the wind to flap a bed-sheet over
your shirt; pray for what you understand.

# SCOPE
(at the movies)

I.
Maybe the future is just
our mood thrown forward
like girls' hair, bleaching at the beach—

After my father's heart attack
his doctor told us,

"This man—he smokes and drinks.
He's heavy. Won't listen. Won't live long.
You should prepare yourselves."

But the doctor suffered depression
(we learned later)
predicting all his patients would die.

My father lived on and on: I can still see him,
heavy, sitting all day sipping Scope mouthwash.

II.
Maybe the future loops around,
a pretzel baking its strands together.

Inside the movie, *Irony of Fate*,
a Soviet bureaucrat gets

so drunk he stumbles onto the wrong train
to the wrong city, wrong building

and apartment . . . yet,
in socialist magical sameness,

his door key fits, and the shocked girl
living there doesn't throw him out.

III.
We squint to see ahead;
whatever's out there jumps and blurs
the lens—

In a movie of the future, a border guard,
Colonel Harper, escapes his earth station

after his witty British wife is blown up.
He meets and beats up another Colonel Harper,

his own cloned double,
then flies to that clone's earth station,

where he confronts his same witty wife,
also cloned, and continuing the same

domestic argument they had at breakfast . . .
Harper ascends, and nukes the great sky pyramid.

IV.
On the skull's blank-white screen,
the movie plots curve and reel,
a future like the forgotten past—

Now it's the guardian Major Cage
who saves the world a hundred times.

He's caught in a time-loop
and can only escape by learning

how to kill the Invaders.
Each time Cage fails, a witty

British girl shoots him in the head,
sending him back to the start. *Blackout.*

V.
—Our doctor swam in sickness, so to him
everyone looked sick.

—The Russian girl had never met
the drunk before, so they got along fine.

—Harper, the cloned man, blew the world to bits
rather than quarrel at breakfast forever.

—Each time Cage fails, a witty
British girl shoots him in the head,
sending him back. *Blackout.*

VI.
Now and always, over over,
the ancient stories, and hair thrown forward.

My father is always drunk,
Scope is 19% alcohol.
—When do I wake up?

He fails, a witty
British girl shoots him in the head . . . .

Memory, and the bracing gunshots,
bounce around the room.

II

### Select Characteristics of U.S. Iron & Steel Mill Injuries & Illnesses with Days Away from Work (2008)

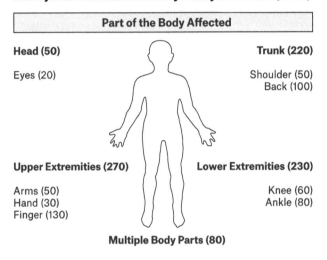

**Part of the Body Affected**

**Head (50)**

Eyes (20)

**Trunk (220)**

Shoulder (50)
Back (100)

**Upper Extremities (270)**

Arms (50)
Hand (30)
Finger (130)

**Lower Extremities (230)**

Knee (60)
Ankle (80)

**Multiple Body Parts (80)**

http://www.in.gov/dol/files/QMS_Iron_and_Steel_Mills_Brochure.pdf

# FORT NECESSITY
## a poem in documents

MY FIRST AUTOPSY: AGE TEN

A man walked into EMERGENCY, dropped dead.
His body was a garden my father tilled,

blade ploughing the flesh, seeking his death:
what part of his life had killed him?

My father grasped dead arms: *This is a working man.*
Little helper, I touched the puzzle of his hand—

ruts and scorch-marks, yellow-brown nicotine
nails, map of the defiant edifice, yielding

from the heart's glutted tube, a black crumb
my father took for death . . . .

> He made me witness
> unspeakable injury
> cut my childhood
> under its blank sheet

---

## BIRTH RACKET

Baby born for it. 12-hour workday,
seven days a week. Through the drum-skin
of its mother's womb, it rocks to the whir
of machines: iron rain. Swaddled in

factory rags, toddling among forests
of spindles, the racket echoing
its natal home, till it casts off childish things—
at age six—and takes its place on the line:

a wage-man, a snuff sniffer, on whose shoulders
the factory teeters and grows. To speak of
child slavery is to set everyone else working:

mill owners send their lobbyists
to dandle toys before the legislature,
lawyers are sent to suckle the courts . . . .

*Mother Jones*
magazine


## ARBEIT

The animal is one with his activity.
The worker puts his life into the object;
Then his life belongs to the object.

Karl Marx

## THE LORDS OF LABOR

The Law of Competition,                          Andrew Carnegie, 1889
concentration of business
in the hands of the few, is
essential to the progress of the race . . .

I want my fair share, and that's all of it.          Charles Koch, 1989

I can hire one half of the working class          Jay Gould, 1886
to kill the other half.

---

## MY SILENCE, $5.50

July 2, 1972: Ann Arbor Police raided an unli-
censed home for juvenile delinquents today, af-
ter complaints of loud music and noise. Twelve
minors were taken to Social Services. One teen
was released, a temporary worker hired to clean
the home's detention room. He would not
speak with reporters.

*

I walked past the staring boys, unlocked the basement room.
Shag rug of piss, Cheerios, ripped magazines,
underwear, burnt ceiling tiles. Smeared in brown
on the door:
                    *SO ?*
*Rip out the rug,* they said, *Clean all surfaces,*
*and don't talk to anyone.* I knew about this place.

Three days' work, at $5.50/hr.

# CARNEGIE

## LOCKING OUT THE WORKERS

As soon as men realize that
they must seek work elsewhere,
they will melt away
like snow in the summer.

Carnegie to H. C. Frick,
during Homestead Lockout

## BROKEN LABOR SONNET

One of the worker ants, busy at its task,
twitches and scampers off. It starts
to eat at itself—the cordyceps fungus
has infiltrated its body and its mind; now

*Planet Earth*, BBC

it directs the ant to crawl upward, high up,
to grip its mandibles upon a stem,
anchor itself and die, becoming soil
for the fruiting body of cordyceps

growing, erupting triumphantly
from the ant-head, a long furry stalk
heavy with spores, that burst above

the colony, filter down, wipe it out . . .

(but in Henry Clay Frick's dream)

—Those infected, if discovered
by other workers, are quickly dragged away
and dumped far from the colony.


PITTSBURGH CENTURY: A LEDGER

1792:  first blast furnace.
1840s: blister spring, plow steel, puddling furnace, pig iron.
1872:  Bessemer process. Andrew Carnegie starts steel production.
1890:  Sherman Anti-Trust Act.
1892:  Carnegie Associations: blast, iron and steel rolling mills,
         Bessemer, open hearth, cold rails, armor plate, bridge-iron,
         wire and wire nails, gas, ore, and coke mines—
1892:  Homestead: steel workers locked out by Carnegie & Frick.


DUMB HUNKIES

*Do you smell gas?*
"You stay li'l bit, pretty soon you drunk.
You stay li'l bit more, pretty soon you dead."

Charles Walker, *Diary of a Furnace Worker*

Molten slag spills from a giant ladle—
lugs don't fit to the rim: a man is roasted,
becomes a steel-man.

Pit boss's orders confuse a Slavic worker.
"By God these Hunkies are dumb."

One in four immigrants, injured or killed at work.
*My lungs were paper on fire.*


PORTRAIT OF A WORK TOURIST

MONROE POWER, off the I-75,
grandest of coal-burning power plants—

hard-hats feed the turbines queen jelly,
soot of Egyptian tombs coating the floors.

The building shakes; it kills a man every year,
and lights the asthma wards of those it made sick;

OSHA forced Monroe to sweep itself clean.              when the union refused
We merry band of day-workers, we drudge-men,           the work, we came in

skinkers, and schlubs. *Sweep out the place,*
a foreman hands us brooms. *Come back at 4.*

—But soft, here are chairs hidden behind lockers:
our elders hide there all day playing

bid whist, slapping down cards and cursing.
One sentry is posted outside: someone 17

and innocent of cards. *Boy, until you can play,*
*you have to work.* I push the silt from left to right,

and right to left . . . the slow servile hours,
the dust sealing to my little gray mask.

# HOMESTEAD LOCKOUT

## SATANIC MILLS: EMMA GOLDMAN

It was Homestead, not Russia; I knew it now. Andrew Carnegie conveniently retreated to his Scottish castle, leaving Henry Clay Frick to negotiate with the striking unions.

He locked them out of Homestead mill, and fortified it.
A declaration of war.

Labor throughout the country was aroused, native toilers had risen!

**FAMILIES OF STRIKERS EVICTED
FROM COMPANY HOUSES.**

At night, a barge packed with strike-breakers and armed Pinkerton thugs slaughtered the steel-workers.

**FIERCE BATTLES AT THE STEEL WORKS
TEN MEN KILLED AND FIFTY WOUNDED.**

The time for our manifesto passed. Innocent blood, the psychological moment for an *Attentat*. "I will kill Frick," Sasha Berkman said, "and give my life for the people." I hung on his lips.

PITTSBURG, JULY 6. — Mob law prevailed at *New York Times* Homestead to-day. The Carnegie Steel Works strikers fought an organized and disciplined force of 300 Pinkerton men, and gained a signal victory. The Pinkerton men surrendered, and will be held to answer the charge of murder.

New York. Sixty dollars left. Sasha needed twenty dollars more for a gun and a suit of clothes.

## ANARCHIST ON THE STREETS Emma Goldman

I woke knowing how to raise money for Sasha.
I would go on the street.

I recollected Dostoyevsky's *Crime and Punishment*: Sonya became a prostitute to support her family and relieve her consumptive stepmother of worry—

Could I attract men on the street? I inspected my body. Tired, but my complexion was good. Curly blonde hair, blue eyes; large in the hips (Jewish stock). Corsets, high heels, dainty underwear, linen dress, Caucasian embroidery . . .

I walked up and down 14th St., in the procession of girls. The vulgar glance of men made me hop away. A distinguished man of sixty approached: "Let's have a drink, little girl."

He scrutinized me as we sat. "You're a novice in the business. I've watched you, you're not here for looseness or excitement."

This made me resentful:
*"Girls are driven here by economic necessity!"*
I wanted to discuss the Social question, my ideas.

He stopped me: "You haven't got the knack for prostitution, that's that." And handed me $10. "Go home. Your dress doesn't match your shoes. You're a child."

"I was twenty-three last month," I protested.

He grinned. The simplicity of his manner pleased me. I asked his name and address, to return his money someday. He refused:

"I love mysteries." He held my hand, and then we parted.                    *Living My Life*

### CHAIRMAN FRICK SHOT

———

*DESPERATE CRIME OF A RUSSIAN ANARCHIST.*

———

### TWO BULLETS ENTER THE BODY OF MR. FRICK — STABBED TWICE IN STRUGGLE TO DISARM ASSAILANT — HIS WOUNDS NOT FATAL.

PITTSBURG, PENN., July 23. — The labor troubles in Allegheny County culminated to-day in a desperate attempt to assassinate H. C. Frick, Chairman of the Carnegie Steel Co. The would-be assassin is a New-York crank whose name, so far as the police are able to learn, is Simon Bachman.                    *New York Times*

Sewn up, Frick returned to work,
then was carried out by stretcher.

His father, an angry Mennonite,
once hung a motto:

"If you want to know who's boss,
just start something."

CARNEGIE: WEALTH GOSPEL

Wealth, passing through the hands
of the few, becomes the property
of the many, ensuring the survival
of the fittest in every department.

There are higher uses for surplus wealth
than adding petty sums to the earnings
of the masses . . . frittered away in things
pertaining to the body and not the spirit:

richer food and drink, better clothing,
more extravagant living. Things external
and of the flesh . . . .

LEDGER AFTER HOMESTEAD: EARNED & SPENT

1892–1899: Value of Carnegie products: +226%.
        Percent of revenues paid to workers: −67%.

1892: men who lifted, hauled, and shoveled.
1899: scooping machines, automatic car dumpers,
        barrows, electric trolleys, overhead cranes—
        Workforce reduction: 25%.

1901: Carnegie Steel sold to JP Morgan; becomes US Steel.
        Andrew Carnegie, "the richest man in the world."

NIETZSCHEAN:

"This is the hardest of all:
To close the open hand out of love"—

1883–1929: Carnegie libraries funded: 2,509.
Carnegie funds given to the poor: 0.

überman of charity
and deprivation

CAN

The next summer I collected garbage, working Route 2
"with the other college boy," a grad student researching Labor.
Burly guy, he could lift.  He said,

"After a year carrying cans, I see the body breaking down:
a couple of hernias, then just hope you become a driver.
A guy died last week. I dressed up for the funeral,
but the whole crew was totally decked out! Silk and satin. . . .

I can write on labor sociology. I'm no tourist here.
But I don't know the first fucking thing about these men."

# CONVICTIONS: SLAVERY AFTER SLAVERY

KOCH, THE NUTCRACKER                                David Koch, 2010

*The Nutcracker* is a ballet that keeps on giving.
It's the money-maker . . .


WORKING THE FLESH                                   US Dept. of Labor

From 1902 to 1907, *The Factory Inspector*,
unofficial journal of the International Association
of Factory Inspectors, published accounts
of industrial accidents. Butler, PA:

a heavy pot of molten steel poured on
two workmen, literally cooking them. Caught
in a shafting, a boy working in a coffin plant
was decapitated, and limbs cut off.

Philadelphia Caramel Works:
Martin Stoffel was sliced into small pieces.
Then, a curious coincidence:
two men called John Minick, unrelated,

working in different cities, working the same
day and hour, were each killed when their clothing
was caught in rotating shafting.
No one witnessed either accident.                    but the Dept.
                                        remembers an interesting death

## SOCIAL CONTRACT SONG

Work all week an' don' make enough                    sung by Lemuel Jones
Pay my board an' buy my snuff.


What you gonna do when the liquor gives out,
A-standing on the corner with your mouth poked out . . .


Sweet thing, sweet thing, sweet thing—              Leroy Allen, Cummins
Danced all night with a bottle in my hand,          Prison Farm, Arkansas
A-looking for the woman ain't got no man . . . .


The Judge he found me guilty, boys,                 Howard Horne
And the clerk he wrote it down;                     (Alan Lomax recordings)
He turned me over to the contractor,
And I'm penitentiaree-bound.



## PRISON: INDUSTRY

The Warden was censured by the Inspectors           Alexander Berkman,
because of the reduced profits from the industries.  *Prison Memories of*
Now the tasks are increased; even the sick          *an Anarchist*
and consumptives are forced to work.


Outside the prison, the labor bodies of the State
protest in vain. How miserably weak they are:
the Giant of Toil, unconscious of his strength!

## LUCKY 13TH

Neither slavery nor involuntary servitude,  Thirteenth Amendment
*except as a punishment for crime whereof*
*the party shall have been duly convicted,*
shall exist within the United States . . . .


## IRON HEAD GOSPEL

—Oh did you hear  sung by James (Iron Head) Baker,
   What the captain said?  Central State Farm Prison, Texas

That if you work
   He'll treat you well
And if you don't
   He'll give you hell.

Oh, long-time man,
   Hold up your head.
Well, you may get a pardon,
   And you may drop dead.

Our jails are money-making machines.                    Prison inspector, 1922

---

*Race*: Negro.    *Sex*: Male.
*Skin*: Gray.    *Age*: 51, 28, 73, 17 . . .

*Name of Crime*: ~~Not given~~. Vagrancy, Eavesdropping.

*Sentence*:  Fine, $5 or 10 days Hard Labor.
              Unable to pay Fine, Court fees. 104 days Hard Labor.
              (refer, Alabama Convict Leasing System.)

*Worksite*:  lean-to shelter in Pine forest (Turpentine Extraction.)
*Worksite*:  Cage rolling on rail tracks built by Convicts.
*Worksite*:  Comer Plantation, Eureka Mines,
              Gov. B. B. Comer, J. W. Comer, *proprietors*.

*Bad Conduct*: Refusal to Work. *Discipline*: 12 Lashes.

*Cause of death*: Killed by Convict, Asphyxia from Explosion,
                  Tuberculosis, Burned by Gas Explosion,
                  Pneumonia, Shot by Foreman,
                  Gangrenous Appendicitis,
                  Paralysis—

                                        Alabama State Report, 1918

---

We are paying the State a great big price          President, Tennessee Coal Co.,
for these convicts, and it is certainly a hardship   subsidiary of US Steel,
on us to deplete our numbers of men.               formerly Carnegie Steel

We think US Steel proper was a positive player     Thomas Ferrall,
in this history . . . a force for good.             US Steel, 2001

41

COMERS, MY BROTHERS

J. W. Comer is a hard man.  I have seen him hit men          Letter, Ezekiel Archey
100 to 160 times with a ten prong strop
and then say thay was not whipped.


The chief inducement for the hiring of convicts              Tennessee Coal Co.
was the certainty of a supply of coal for
our manufacturing operations in the                          meaning,
contingency of labor troubles.                               prisoners v. unions


We are outraged at the attempts to establish                 Gov. B. B. Comer,
social equality between black and white miners . . .         owner, Eureka Mines
We will not tolerate eight or nine thousand
idle niggers in the state of Alabama.


A keen scrutiny of the bookkeeping practices                 Alabama Governors
and greater accountability in general                        archive
were applied to the state's convict lease system


    [  language  language  ]


efficient administration of the convict system
net the state of Alabama near $400,000 per year . . .        most of state income



ENTERRAR Y CALLAR                                            Goya, *Los desastres
                                                             de la guerra*

Bury them, and keep quiet

---

## LOCKED RAILWAY CAR, BOTTOM OF MOUNTAIN

Right off the boat from Ellis Island, we saw the sign:

**FREE TRAIN TO BROOKLYN.**

The doors lock, the train takes us instead to Brooklyn, West Virginia. A
coal town, a Company town: scrips, store, and shanty; debt, and no road
out. My English so bad, I thought "mine" meant "me."

> What became of us? Give us a name:
> blacksmith, motorman, tipple-boy and spragger.
> Car trimmer, slate dumper, brattice and pumpman—
> Nights, we chip in for booze at the boss's Store.

> My lady, we have lived here by month
> and lifetime, our babies grown and gone
> to the mines. We are always looking up;
> but now the house falls on our heads.

The Bureau says, "Even if workers demand them, unsanitary shacks should
not be built." Then they visit us: "Part of camp at bottom of mountain,
but drainage excellent."

But I say:

"not fit to live in most evry house leakes and the workmens Bed clothing
are spoiled evry nait."                                    Local Union No. 2839

ETYMOLOGIES:

*Slave (n.) Quatrain*

Middle English sclave, from Old French esclave,      *The Free Dictionary*
from Medieval Latin sclāvus, *Slav:*
*from the widespread enslavement*
*of Slavs in the early Middle Ages.*      and Frank means *free*

*New Century Man*

1912: Ioseb Besarionis Dze Jugashvili
takes the name Josef Stalin.
Stalin: *Man of Steel.*

44

# ROCKEFELLER

NO. I

Rockefeller, you know—                                                        William James

flexible, cunning, quakerish . . .
        a thickset animal;
a man 10 stories deep
        and quite unfathomable—

A sleeve with a fist sewn up inside.                                          Victor Hugo

It's the only dream you can have—                                    *Death of a Salesman*
To come out number-one man.

DOLL

The thing about a shark is                                                   from *Jaws*
he's got lifeless eyes—
black eyes. Like a doll's eyes.
When he comes at you,
he doesn't even seem to be living—
till he bites you, and
those black eyes roll over white . . . .

OILMAN LEDGER

1850: Rockefeller, age 10, divides pound candy,
      sells smaller portions to his siblings for profit.
1859: Rockefeller pays for a slave's freedom.
      Oil gushes: Titusville, Pothole, Oil City, PA.
1882: Standard Oil's secret "Trust of Nine" creates 34 companies:
      oil refining, pipes, barrels, storage, transit, credit, sales—
1890: Sherman Anti-Trust Act. Standard controls 88% of market.
1911: Standard Oil declared monopoly, is broken into 90 companies.
      John D. Rockefeller, "the richest man in the world."


My *Ledger A* . . . almost brought tears to my eyes.     John D. Rockefeller


RAILWAY SQUEEZE SONNET                          Letters, independent
                                                oil producers

"A Standard Oil-man from your city
    followed that oil car
and oil to my place, and told me
    he would not let me

make a dollar on that oil,
    dogging me around
for two days to buy Standard Oil,
    making all sorts of threats . . . ."

"If I get a barrel of oil out of Buffalo
    I have to *sneak* it out.
The railroads control the docks
    and they won't let me out:

They are all afraid of offending
the Standard Oil Company."

## FROM ROCKEFELLER'S THROAT

[ language ] ... we bought the largest and best refineries
  and centralized their administration, securing
  greater economy and efficiency, reducing

  the cost of transportation for both the railroads
  and ourselves.  All this was following
  in the natural laws of trade.


## NATURAL LAW CHORUS

The wonderful progress of the United States,                    Charles Darwin
as well as the character of the people,
are the results of natural selection.

Rockefeller ... plays beautifully                               William James
with his grandchild, carrying her on his back,
he wrecks businesses, ruins widows and orphans ...

Will you tell me how to prevent luxury                          John Adams, letter
from producing effeminacy, intoxication,                        to Thomas Jefferson
extravagance, Vice and folly?


## ROCKEFELLER AT HOME                                          Ida Tarbell, *History*
                                                                *of Standard Oil*

Family and servants trained to strictest economy.
No more gas burned than is needed, no unnecessary
heating, no wasteful providing—

Concealment, a Chinese wall of seclusion,
diet of the pauper and the monk.
Nothing for display, nothing squandered in
the senseless American way to prove you are rich.


HIS EYES                                                    Ida Tarbell


Small and intent and steady, they are as expressionless as a wall.

   They see everything and reveal nothing.
   Not a shifty eye—not a cruel or leering one,
   but something vastly more to be feared—

   a blank eye, looking through and through things,
   telling nothing of what they found . . . .

   Forever peering into hidden places,
   for money, always more money, planning
   in secret to wrest it even from his friends,
   never forgetting, never resting, never satisfied—


RUDE MECHANICALS: A MEDLEY

Some man or other must present Wall:                    *A Midsummer*
and let him have some plaster, or some loam,            *Night's Dream*
or some rough-cast about him, to signify wall . . .
Tell them plainly: he is Snug the Joiner.

   Don't leave oil in pipes—                       Rockefeller
   10,000 good barrels on hand:
   Coopers must work *more*.

Look over yonder on Jericho's wall                    Spiritual
    Rocks and mountains, don't fall on me
And see those sinners tremble and fall
    Rocks and mountains, don't fall on me


CORPORATE HEAD: ALOPECIA                    Ida Tarbell

The disease has swept Mr. Rockefeller's head
bare of hair, stripped away even his eyelashes and eyebrows,
has revealed all the strength of his

    great head, curious bumps and tightly drawn,
    dry naked skin.


HIS MOUTH                    Ida Tarbell

Its former mask, the full mustache, is now completely gone.
Indeed the greatest loss Mr. Rockefeller sustained when
his hair went was that it revealed his mouth . . .

    It is only a slit—
    the lips are quite lost, as if by eternal
    grinding together of the teeth—
    teeth set on something he would have . . . .

    It is at once the cruelest feature of his face—
    this mouth—

    the cruelest and the most pathetic, for the hard,
    close-set line slants downward at the corners,
    giving a look of age and sadness.

PAPER ENVOI

Ash father,

your autopsies stamped a thousand tokens—
DYSENTERY   STROKE   CANCER   POISON—
and built a counting-house for death,
till your own death bewildered you
and stole back the secrets
of its enterprise.

Now, I have brought you treasures:
steel-men roasted, chopped up, shot;
oil-men gushing, mouth of smoke and fire;
coal-miners breathing their graves.
The body, a tool wearing down,

a saw breaking its teeth. And here too
sits the sleepless owner,
hunched over his meal of numbers,
bloodshot, fingers worrying his face:

Godsbody and target.

My creased papers form
a roof for your house underground;
tears and terrors and blood—mere ink.
Will you read a pattern in their lives,
will their deaths puzzle you again?

# THE FORT

## THE COMPANY WAR-TRAIL

A deer-path, a moccasin-path along the ridge,
quick movements of paper birch . . . French scouts;

Nemacolin's Path along the Monongahela River,
nation's vein flowing to the Ohio valley, 1754.

On behalf of the *Ohio Land Company*, Gov. Dinwiddie (an investor), sends Col. George Washington to widen the path for Company
settlers:

*Make Prisoners of or kill all who obstruct the Works.*

Washington half-drowns, the Allegheny is thick with ice; clambers
onto Wainwrights Island, at the Forks of the Ohio River . . .

Nemacolin's Path: now US 40, *The National Highway*. Wainwrights
Island: now 40th St., Pittsburgh, PA.

## PATRICIDE. "A CHARMING FIELD."

Washington and *Half-King*, his Mingo friend, lead scouts to ambush
a French encampment. A dozen French killed; Washington and
wounded Capt. de Jumonville parley

but *Half-King*, a former child-slave
sold by the French, comes up
behind Jumonville, whispering

*Tu n'es pas encore mort, mon père*—
not dead yet—and tomahawks his head,
washing his hands in Jumonville's brains—

Washington races back to Great Meadows, makes a rough stockade:
*Fort Necessity*, built in haste. "The soldiers thus employed, and the
bane of idleness avoided"—

In heavy rain, the French attack: entrenchments swamped, powder
wet, muskets useless. Washington signs a surrender, not reading the
clause admitting his

*assassination de M. Jumonville,*

document that sparks the French & Indian War
fought in America, Africa, India, Philippines—
the first world war.

*al cementerio*
—Goya

Horace Walpole, in Parliament:
*a young Virginian has set the world on fire*—

July 4, 1754: Washington's only surrender, age 22. His troops break
into *Fort Necessity* and drink all the rum. The French rob them on
their way out.

Col. Washington:

Letter to his mother

"I have heard the bullets whistle; and believe me, there is
something charming in the sound."

"I have no view of acquisition but to serve my King

*Life & Writings*

and country. We could drive the French from the Ohio,
but our pay would not be sufficient."

---

18TH-CENTURY TRAVEL: WEAR THE YELLOW BADGE!

That the said beggars should be

Jonathan Swift,
"Badges for Beggars"

   confined to their own parishes;
that they should wear badges well
   sewn upon their shoulder,

even then

always visible, on pain of being whipped
   and turned out of town,
or whatever legal punishment may be
   thought proper and effectual.

What shall we do with foreign beggars,
   must they be left to starve?
No, I answer; but they must be driven
   or whipped out of town—

and let the next country parish do as they please.

## 19TH-CENTURY OHIO VALLEY: THE BOSS

Back in eighteen-o-three
James and Danny Heaton
Found the ore that was linin' Yellow Creek—
They built a blast furnace
Here along the shore
And they made the cannonballs
That helped the Union win the war.

Bruce Springsteen,
"Youngstown"

## DAY LABOR, LIGHT DENIED

Lincoln, c. 1861:
"He was the most perfect democrat,
revealing in every word and act
the equality of men."

Carnegie, telegraph
worker for Lincoln

The American Civil War:
a war over hiring
your servants for life,
or just by month and year.

Thomas Carlyle

# SURVIVORS

Tell his life like it was.                          Margaret Carnegie Miller
I'm sick of the Santa Claus stuff.


## LOVE AND DEATH LEDGER

1864: Herbert Spencer's phrase "survival of the fittest."
1882: Carnegie shows Spencer the Pittsburgh steel works;
       Spencer's honorary dinner at Delmonico's restaurant.
1891: All of Rockefeller's hair falls out.
1896: Connecticut outlaws marriage between
       the "epileptic, imbecile, or feeble-minded."
1898: Carnegie offers to purchase the independence of
       the Philippines for $20 million.
1914: Assassination of Archduke Ferdinand sparks WW I.


## METAL LOVE SONNET

"Grapple them unto thy soul with hoops of steel."        Polonius

Swimming in liquid pig metal, hissing in heat        Sir Henry Bessemer
turned violet, orange, and pure white,
are the atoms silicon, carbon, manganese:
each of them loves some atom of oxygen—

Inside the converting-vessel, these lovers meet
and marry. With noisy celebration, the pairs
emerge as globules of atoms and air
soaring radiant from the 12-ton mouth,

spending a short life together,
soft floating specks of bluish light—
a predestination of matter
not found in theologies . . .

(Then, to solidify the steel,
shovel in some spiegelseisen.)


SURVIVAL IN FRAGMENTS: HERBERT SPENCER

My hands are unusually small—smaller than a woman's hands. How is
this? My father and grandfather did nothing more than wield the pen.
Occasionally, my father went fishing . . .

My hands, the result of two generations of diminished activity.

> His manuscript strapped to the waistcoat.
> *Cerebral circulation* problems;
> published the *Principles of Psychology*,
> then had a nervous breakdown.

Waiter, I did not ask for Cheshire; I asked for Cheddar. *Cheddar*.

With prudence . . . my dose of opium (1 or 2 grains) . . .
a wretched night, no sleep, kept in room all day.

> At night he soaks his head in brine,
> covers hair with a flannel cap,
> then to keep the moisture in,
> another, waterproof cap—

The evil caused by the parish fostering the vicious and good-for-nothing: idiots, imbeciles, drunkards, lunatics, paupers, and prostitutes . . . . Women with many bastards are preferred as wives to modest women.

My celibate life, best for me . . . best for some unknown other.

My hands are unusually small— *How is this?*

The repulsiveness of Pittsburgh . . . six months there would justify suicide. At Delmonico's restaurant, I got friends to secrete me in an ante-room so that I might avoid all excitements of introductions and congratulations . . . Great fear I should collapse.

An Autobiography

> Poor, probable, uninteresting         Oscar Wilde
> human life—tired of repeating herself
> for the benefit of Mr. Herbert Spencer.

---

**DINNER IN HONOR OF MR. HERBERT SPENCER.**
DELMONICO'S RESTAURANT, NEW-YORK.

~

*Course Three*
Buttery scarlet kettle-drum-shaped pastry tufts
stuffed with truffles,
tongue, and pistachios

*Course Four*
Striped bass garnished with blanched oysters,
mushroom heads, pike dumplings
and trussed crawfish . . .

---

"higher uses for surplus<br>wealth"—Carnegie

## SPENCER'S AFTER-DINNER SPEECH

And now that I have thanked you,
sincerely though too briefly,
I am going to find fault with you . . .

Your hair turns gray ten years
before ours. . . . Nervous collapse;
friends kill themselves by overwork;

Business, substituted
for war as the purpose of existence.
Everywhere, the faces tell in strong lines

the burdens they have borne. . . . You have
too much of the gospel of work—
Be a boy as long as you can.


## ROCKEFELLER, THE MUMMY

I am *bound* to be rich.                                        said at age 27

Don't be a good fellow. Every downfall                         Rockefeller, speaking
is traceable directly or indirectly                            at Sunday school
to the victim's good cheer among
his friends, who come as quickly as they go—

He is restless, searching the church                           Ida Tarbell
aisles right and left,
and craning his neck
*to see what is behind.* Fear, fear

of the oft-repeated threats
of the multitude of sufferers
from the wheels of the cars
of progress—

Brought face to face with
Mr. Rockefeller unexpectedly,
and not knowing him,
the writer's immediate thought is,

*This is the oldest man in the world—*
*a living mummy.*


TUMULT: 1919

Dec. 2: death of H. C. Frick;
"Frick, deported by God."                                    Alexander Berkman

Dec. 3: ORDER OF DEPORTATION for                            J. Edgar Hoover
Berkman and Goldman, a US citizen,

"two of the most dangerous
anarchists in this country."

Incendiary or bigot could be found—                         W. B. Yeats, "Nineteen
Thunder of feet, tumult of images,                          Hundred and Nineteen"
Their purpose in the labyrinth of the wind

## FROM SASHA

Berkman to Goldman, 1901

Dearest Girl:
Luckily the guards took you for
my "sister," though I believe your identity
was suspected after you left the prison.

I know my strange behavior affected you . . .
Your face after all these years—
I could not think, could not speak.

As if my dreams of freedom, the whole
world of the living, were concentrated
in the shiny little trinket
dangling from your watch chain—

I couldn't take my eyes off it,
couldn't keep from playing with it;
it absorbed my whole being . . .

He dies, a suicide, in 1936

## CARNEGIE: THE SURRENDER, WW I

Tell Mr. Carnegie
I'll meet him in Hell,
where we are both going.

Henry Clay Frick

This most exuberant person
changed completely:

Louise Carnegie

his clothes hung loosely around him,
his face became deeply indented,
his zest for mere existence gone:

overnight, on August 4, 1914,
he became an old man.

US Steel annual profits during WW I:
$240,000,000.

*now thrive*
*the armourers*

DEATH AND MERCY, WW II

Dad sang no lullabies, but his war stories
put me to sleep somewhere, the Philippines,

a field hospital near front lines—
Walking to barracks through woods,

he is jumped by Japanese soldiers,
my eyes are closing now,

kills one and rips the other, falling,
then drags him back to the hospital,

stitching up the wounds
he made    me dreaming—

## SPILL-OVER

CHAIN SONNET

Disease unlocks cell after cell—
liberator and trickster
fighting the body's law.

My father's zeal to read its workings
ruined him:
college at 14, chain-smoking,
killing off his boyhood
to make himself a man,

but still, decades after death,
incomplete—

whatever has fallen,
skin-flakes, fumes, shreds
of smoke, broken voices,
gathers in my hands.

PRISON: RETAIL

Cars range like sucklings at the paps
of the MAINE STATE PRISON STORE, tucked below

the guard-tower, and selling trolls and loveseats
branded MSP. Inmates win "patents" to make

the big sellers, earning profits to
"reimburse the State for room and board."

maine.gov/
corrections/industries

Small crimes fall from the evening air:
heroin slips inside with the lumber;

the guard who doled out favorite patents,
now behind bars making coat racks.

Near the parking lot, jags
of sea shells salt the rock face,

where gulls drop crabs to break their backs,
the muscle twitching in its broken purse—

Tourists peck and rattle their coins,
their tires streaking white as they roll away.


RONDEL

    Think a new wheel:
  ↗         ↘
broken by it        build it
  ↖        ↙
    tied to it  ←  run it


CHAPLAIN COG

The chaplain pauses at my cell-door,
to speak encouragement. I am moved,
but my revolutionary traditions
forbid me to express my emotions.

Alexander Berkman

A cog in the machinery of oppression,
he might mistake my gratitude for that
of a fawning convict.


TRUST: KOCH, TIMES, SPIRITUAL, POST

Idealized steel workers, engaged in noble toil . . .
trains running fast and running full.
Onward and upward: everywhere smoke,
rising to form Heaven itself.

"Carnegie" broadcast, WNET (David Koch, trustee)

*Mississippi*: a criminal population
taught habits of regularity and industry—
at the end of their terms,
eagerly sought by the planters
of the State as laborers.

*New York Times*, 1911

My brother's gone to glory
I want to go there too
Lord, I want to live up yonder
In bright mansions above

Spiritual

The Alabama Department of Corrections
barred an inmate [and library trusty] from ac-
quiring the book *Slavery By Another Name*, a
historical account of the exploitation of black
prisoners, citing Paragraph (V)(G)(4)(a) of
Regulation No. 448: "determined to be a threat
to the security of the institution" . . .

*Washington Post*, 2011

## JOB SONNET

"Got this way in the mines—
We was pumping an old hole dry,
did a record job.  But they
wouldn't give us no stove to dry

Interview by Alan Lomax

our clothes at. At night we'd take off
wet clothes. Next morning, when
we put 'em on, they'd be frozen. Well,
a little wile of that and I couldn't turn

my head.  Boss said: 'You'll get along.'
Three men died of consumption later,
and if I didn't die right away, I been
dying by inches ever since. Look at these hands."

His fingers were yellow, curled like chicken feet,
the flesh of his arms turned into dry pulpy wood.


## ICAHNIC: BROKEN LABOR COUPLETS

Mr. Icahn is worth more than $20 billion,
but management told PSC Metal's union

*New York Times*, 2014

it was dropping their health insurance benefits.
PSC's website: "Our people are our greatest asset."

Union members, who rejected the new terms, were locked out.
"They weren't negotiating. It was take it or leave it"

said Jeff Bryant, who has worked at the yard
for 35 years.

EXTRA, EXTRA

*Good Profit*:                                    book by Charles Koch, 2015
How Creating Value for Others
Built One of the World's Most
Successful Companies

Koch Oil                                          US Senate Report
was engaged in a widespread                       (101-216), 1989
and sophisticated scheme
to steal crude oil from Indians.

———————————————

NO. 1

*It's the only dream you can have—*               *Death of a Salesman*
*To come out number-one man.*

To come outnumber   one man.

WITNESS WITNESS: GUARDING GUARDS                  Witness testimony,
                                                  DC Superior Court
"We were called in, a shoplifter was seen         (David Gewanter,
lifting his security guard jacket and putting     jury member), 2009
meat around his torso; so we stopped him

and there was a lot of tussling and russling,
we had him down but he slung us off
one way and another, then from his sock, pulling

out a steak knife: 'Brother, I'll stab you *up.*'
But we got him down, blood from the steaks
all over his face, and deli meats spilling on the rugs."

# BODY OF WORK

I.
A man had walked into EMERGENCY, dropped dead.
Did his family think he staggered out drunk?
His body was a garden my father tilled,
blade ploughing the flesh, seeking his death:
what part of his life had killed him?
My father grasped dead arms: *This is a working man.*
Little helper, I touched the puzzle of his hand.
*
I touched the puzzle of his hand. Little helper
to my father's work, grasping dead arms
of a man who walked into EMERGENCY, dropped dead.
My father ploughed his flesh, destroyed his own health.
Did our family know he staggered out drunk—
What part of his life had killed him?
The garden is starving; their bodies fill it.

II.
When he fell it was no moral
or metaphor, but a new agreement:
you butcheries and bursting fields,

dry springs, eggs, wrinkling grapes,
all that dies to keep me alive—
here I am, pelt, stew, trophy, savory soil,

all that I have made
of myself . . . .

So when Dr. Gottfried Benn, the decadent poet-doctor,
pried opened the corpse's mouth,
he found a flower caught in the teeth.

Broke open the chest, planted it there—
*drink up, little aster!*—
and sewed the satchel closed.

A day,
torn light, another day, and then

we dry up, become a second food—
rind, gristle, raisin, or pickle;
fat drippings for gravy,
the scum on boiling milk; or the burnt specks

clinging to the plate when the pie is eaten,
when the maker, still hungry, leans down
to scratch for crumbs.

III

# THE LORDS OF LABOR
—Karl Marx writing "The Economic and Philosophic Manuscripts of 1844"


It was the time when children scrubbed
        inside chimneys, or crawled
    the methane swamps of the coal mines,

lit by iridescent fish.
        Mud streets and snuff and muck slops,
    horsehair beds, grindwheel and harrow.

The time when *to show your mettle*
        meant showing the flint chips
    stuck in your arm; when

*to fire a worker* meant, burn down his house.

~


Time was, Karl Marx sat rubbing his back
        (no bristling beard yet; no doctrines),
    sat studying so long

he couldn't sit; the doctor said he'd gotten
        *Weaver's Bottom*, new ailment
    of the kitchen-industrial age.

Marx frowns at his Hegel. Hegel's ideas
        flutter like angels overhead.
    Lonely, he watches the fire grate;

the flames dancing . . . such indolence.
      A philosopher can see, in
      the burning branch, a devil-shape.

*The worker puts his life into the object;*
      *his life belongs to the object;*
      *then the owner takes up the object.*

Worker and owner, fighting for the beloved—
      a tale of Romance.
      *When a man's work is torment,*

*the owner feels pleasure . . .*
      The pages eddy in Marx's hands
      and shift along his body.

~

A time when skull-lumps were measured,
      when hot bottles pressed to the skin
      sucked out disease. The mind,

its offices and strong-rooms, littered with stories.
      The tongue, restless in the mouth;
      the fingers grip the pen like a spike—

Charles Dickens holds up *Tale of Two Cities*:
      "What is done and suffered
      in these pages

I have done and suffered myself."
      His novel splits him into
      two parts, twenty, hundreds:

Dickens becomes both hero and lout,
      the golden-breasted girl
      and the vengeful, knitting Madame;

is Jerry Cruncher digging up corpses,
      so the body can labor after death,
      showing itself to students . . . .

~

*Who are the lords of labor,*
      the lords of cure and crime—
      the owners? Or the working body,

the broken mold of its work:
      a stonegrinder's arm, heavy
      with flecks of stone; a farmer's thumb,

swollen red with fertilizer.
      (The almanac lists the ailments as
      *Mettle. Farmer's Thumb.*)

The cop by the highway,
      speed-gun in his lap
      humming with cancer—

Say goodbye to what you have made,
      watch your child flee from home;
      wave and wave and wait for your coin

to drop like mercury into the palm,
      nestling in divots and cuts,
      passing through flesh . . . .

~

Marx shifts painfully. His notes pile up.
        Someday, he becomes homework,
    robbing students of sex and drink.

Only the youngest students are free,
        the children with their big books
    and their helper, the Norfolk terrier:

speak to it, and its head cocks in curiosity,
        as if suffering a pinched nerve—
    the posture called *Wry Neck.*

The terrier is paired with kids
        whose parents are away;
    they read it stories,

to which the terrier tilts wryly,
        "Really? Is that so?"
    And then one child,

thinking they are now friends,
        holds out the book to the dog:
    *Now it's your turn. Read my story,*

and the dog head bows on its slender stalk.

# NOTES

"Ruth, the Rocket": "Storm Chasing on Saturn," *New York Times*, August 6, 2014.

"Scope": "Harper: in the movie," *Oblivion* (2013).

"Cage: in the movie," *Edge of Tomorrow* (2014).

"Survivors": Spencer material from Deckle Edge's *Banquet at Delmonico's* (New York: Random House, 2009).

"Prison: Industry": "Thousands of ICE Detainees Claim They Were Forced into Labor: A Violation of Anti-slavery Laws," *Washington Post*, March 5, 2017.

CPSIA information can be obtained
at www.ICGtesting.com
Printed in the USA
BVHW04s0145230418
514049BV00001B/13/P

9 780226 533766